Some Assembly Required

Poems to Bless, Inspire and Comfort

REGINA A. SOLLERS

TEACHABLE MOMENTS
PRESS
Elkridge, Maryland

Some Assembly Required

Copyright © 2016 Regina A. Sollers
All rights reserved

All scripture references in this book are from the King James Version of the Bible @1994 by the Zondervan Corporation.

SOME ASSEMBLY REQUIRED

ISBN-13: 978-0-9905811-2-3
ISBN-10: 0990581128
Second Edition Printed in the United States of America

PRESS

Teachable Moments Press
6030 Marshalee Drive, #175
Elkridge, MD 21075
www.teachablemomentspress.com

Library of Congress Control Number: 2016961262

No part of this book may be reproduced or transmitted in any form or by any means electronic or mechanical—including photocopying, recording, or by any information storage and retrieval system—without permission in writing from the publisher, except as provided by United States of America Copyright Law. Please direct your inquiries to permissionseditor@teachablemomentspress.com

TO MY READERS

It is my desire that you will be blessed beyond measure as you read the poems God has inspired me to write. I pray that they will encourage, inspire and comfort you in some way. Thanks for your patronage and may God richly bless you.

Poems to Bless, Inspire and Comfort

CONTENTS

Acknowledgments	i - iii
GENERAL POEMS	1
Today Is a Blessed Day	2
I See What You're Trying to Do, Lord	4
Delayed Time	6
Yes, I'm Alive	9
Young Man, Young Man	10
When The Door Slams Shut	12
A Treasure	16
Somebody Ought to Know	18
As Long As You Have King Jesus	20
The Appointment	24
The Dress	26
Freedom For All	29
Some Assembly Required	30

LOVE POEMS 33

We Did it God's Way	34
Blessed Love	36
I'm Drawn To You	38
Endless Love	40
I Love It When… (the husband)	42
I Love It When… (the wife)	46
I Am My Beloved's and My Beloved is Mine	50
The Proposal	52

TESTIMONIAL POEMS 55

Go Forward	56
Idle Words	59
God is a Teacher	62
Obey God Right Now	64

ABOUT THE AUTHOR 66

ACKNOWLEDGEMENTS

Thanks to God for His direction and guidance in preparing this book.

Thanks to my mom and dad, the late William and Louise Young, for their love and the work ethics they instilled in their children to strive to do our best whatever the task. ***Do all things whole-heartedly as unto God.***

Thanks to my former pastor, the late Bishop George W. Hawkins, Sr. for the many powerful sermons he preached which inspired several of the poems in this book.

And thanks for the various testimonies I heard and observations God allowed me to see. Glory to God!

SPECIAL ACKNOWLEDGEMENTS

I thank God for blessing me with my beautiful daughter Terri T. Jacobs who is a constant joy and amazing woman to me. She is a caring and loving daughter, wife, mother and most recently grandmother.

I also recognize my son-in-law Alphonzo D. Jacobs who shows me the utmost respect and much love. He is a devoted husband, father and affectionate grandfather and an upright example to his children.

Also, I salute my grandchildren Brittney and Aaron who have grown into beautiful and responsible adults. Additionally, I bless God for the latest addition to the family Payton D. Jacobs. He truly is a joy to our family.

I acknowledge my brothers (William, Russell, Edmond and Cordell) and sisters (Sarah, Curly, and Rosia) and their families for their love and support.

Special acknowledgements to my pastor Derek T. Hawkins, his wife Wauketa and their family and my wonderful church family at the Church of God Lothian, Maryland.

*"I delight to do thy will, O my God.
Yea, thy law is within my heart."*

-- Psalm 40:8

GENERAL POEMS

"They that trust in the Lord shall be
as mount Zion,
Which cannot be removed, but
abideth forever.
As the mountains are round about
Jerusalem,
so the Lord is round about his
people
from henceforth even for ever."

-- Psalm 125:1-2

SOME ASSEMBLY REQUIRED

TODAY IS A BLESSED DAY

Today is a Blessed Day

Today is a blessed day just look all around;
a bluer sky cannot be found.
Fluffy white clouds floating above -
oh what a blessing to see God's love.

Sky nice and clear and the sun shining bright -
what a blessing to bask in the flowing sunlight.
As I beheld the beauty of God's great glory;
My mind began to drift to that old redemption story.

Wouldn't it be wonderful on a day just like this—
while every eye behold that heavenly bliss;
the sight of our Lord and Savior appearing in the sky
to take us home to that great bye and bye.

Yes, today is a blessed day just look all around;
a bluer sky cannot be found.
Fluffy white clouds floating above -
oh, what a blessing to see God's love.

(Written August 5, 2004: While on my way to pick up my grandchildren so that we could mow my mom's yard, I noticed the beautiful sky.)

SOME ASSEMBLY REQUIRED

I SEE WHAT YOU'RE TRYING TO DO, LORD

REGINA A. SOLLERS

I See What You're Trying to Do, Lord

You wake me early, get up you say.
Go to a quiet place—to meditate and pray.
Talk to me before you begin your day;
Hurrying and scurrying on your way.

Don't forget to read my Word, I hear you say.
Can I have just ten minutes of your day?
My Word will keep the evil spirits at bay;
And, yes, it will keep your mind from spiritual decay.

I see what you're trying to do, Lord.
Your Word will keep me on one accord.
Yes, I see what you're trying to do, Lord.
Return to you and become entrenched again in your Word.

(After God has given us the desires of our heart, many times we become slack in our prayers and Bible reading. God has a way of telling us that we are not communicating with Him like we should. Don't let the blessings make you forget the Blesser.)

SOME ASSEMBLY REQUIRED

DELAYED TIME

Delayed Time

Don't get complacent because Jesus hasn't returned,
and begin to stray away from the things you have learned.
Don't begin to gossip, backbite and defraud—
continue to pray and put on the full armor of God.

Don't be like the ungrateful Israelites
while Moses was on the mount forty days and nights.
They quickly turned away from the one true God;
from His protection His staff and His rod.

Where is this Moses? When will he return?
And their desire for other gods begin to burn.
So they slipped back into sin and made a golden calf.
But one day God will separate the wheat from the chaff.

Why would you think that the Bible is not true?
When Jesus said He's gone to prepare a place for you.
Yes His return is being delayed
because there are more folks that have to be saved.

SOME ASSEMBLY REQUIRED

Use this time to obey and to do God's will.
Cease to do evil and His commandments fulfill.
Lift up a standard while time is delayed.
Be patient my brother, and give God the praise.

(Inspired by a sermon preached August 23, 2003).

Yes, I'm Alive

Left my Father's house, where everything was grand -
to come to earth and live among sinful man.
To be a perfect example of how to live sin free;
and then to be crucified upon Calvary's tree.

Put in a cold grave and stayed for three days
Then I got up, man's debt was paid.
Went to Galilee, my disciples I needed to see;
To leave them instructions to teach about me.

Ascended to Heaven, where I'm preparing you a place
To be with my Father and to look upon His face.
Yes, I'm alive - watching over you day and night.
Always guiding and directing you to do what's right.

"And it came to pass, while he blessed them, he was parted from them, and carried up into heaven.:"

-- Luke 24:51

SOME ASSEMBLY REQUIRED

YOUNG MAN, YOUNG MAN

Young Man, Young Man

Young man, young man
Why is your life so bleak?
Young man, young man
What is it that you seek?
You walk around with your head hung down;
It makes my heart bleed, to see you in need.
Young man, young man.

Young man, young man
Let me give you a clue.
Young man, young man
This is what you should do.
Look to God, after all He is the one who made you.
Don't you think He knows how to save you?
Young man, young man.

(Written with my Godchild in mind August 31, 1977—January 24, 2003)

"Wherewithal shall a young man cleanse his way? By taking heed thereto according to thy word"

-- Psalm 119:9

SOME ASSEMBLY REQUIRED

WHEN THE DOOR SLAMS SHUT

REGINA A. SOLLERS

When the Door Slams Shut

Where will you be;
when the door slams shut?
Safe with Jesus on the inside
Or weeping and wailing on the outside.

Let me tell you the story about Noah.
He preached 120 years to mankind;
telling them to stop their sinful ways
Or else they would be left behind.

But they continued their wickedness, my friend.
God saw it and said "this has got to end".
So Noah and his family went into the ark
God slammed shut the door and the rain did start.

Do you know the parable of the ten virgins?
Five were wise and five were foolish.
Five had oil for their lamps, and five did not.
So they went to buy because their lamps had gone out.

SOME ASSEMBLY REQUIRED

While they were gone the bridegroom came.
The wise virgins were ready with their lamps aflame.
They went in with Him and the door was shut.
The foolish were left outside; Jesus said, "I know you not".

Watch therefore because we know not the day.
Neither do we know the hour, the Bible does say.
Don't let this happen to you my friend.
When the door is shut this time it will be the end.

> *"And the key of the house of David will I lay upon his shoulder;…and he shall shut, and none shall open."*
>
> -- Isaiah 22:22

> **Dear God,**
> I need you.
> I am humbly calling out to you.
> I'm tired of doing things my way.
> Help me to start doing things your way.
> I invite you into my life to be my Lord and be my Savior.
> Fill the emptiness in me with Your Holy Spirit and make me whole.
> Lord, help me to trust You,
> help me to love You,
> help me to live for You,
> and help me to understand Your grace, Your mercy and Your peace.
> Thank You, Lord.
> In Jesus' name I pray.
> **AMEN.**

Today, I accept Christ into my life as my Lord and Savior.

_____
Signed

Date:_____

SOME ASSEMBLY REQUIRED

A TREASURE

A Treasure

Oh, what a treasure I found
at a yard sale. My eyes were astound.
To my surprise - oh can this be true
the Holy Bible so bright and shiny new.

How much is this Bible, myself I questioned;
as I put it with my other possessions.
Five dollars, you think; or maybe three.
My friend said one or perhaps it's free.

Oh no, I balk this Bible is unused -
so fresh and clean; the pages not abused.
How much for the Bible I softly inquired.
Oh just give me a quarter, the young girl replied.

Quickly I paid her what she asked;
anxious to leave with God's road map.
Does not she realize the treasures present?
In the book she just sold for twenty-five cents.

(Written: Saturday, August 9, 2003)

SOME ASSEMBLY REQUIRED

SOMEBODY OUGHT TO KNOW

Somebody Ought to Know

Somebody ought to know that you are a child of God.
Somebody ought to be able to see the evidence.
Somebody ought to say "there goes a Holy woman".
Somebody ought to know.

Somebody ought to know that you live a godly life.
Somebody ought to be able to tell by your walk.
Somebody ought to say "she is a true woman of God".
Somebody ought to know.

Somebody ought to know that God's Spirit flows within.
Somebody ought to be able to see His image in you.
Somebody ought to say "she's a beautiful person".
Somebody ought to know.

"Let your light so shine before men that they may see your good works, and glorify your father which is in heaven."

-- St. Matthew 5:16

SOME ASSEMBLY REQUIRED

AS LONG AS YOU HAVE KING JESUS, YOU CAN DEAL WITH EVERYTHING ELSE

As Long As You Have King Jesus, You Can Deal With Everything Else

Problems—big or small—weighing you down;
seems so insurmountable, will peace ever be found?
Don't fret and don't despair; be encouraged.
For as long as you have King Jesus,
you can deal with everything else.

Troubles all around seem to have you bound;
laden down with burdens—will joy ever abound?
Look to the hills where your help comes from.
For as long as you have King Jesus,
you can deal with everything else.

Persecuted on all sides—both left and right.
By my brother and my sister who are in Jesus Christ.
But I don't worry and I won't fret.
For as long as I have King Jesus,
I can deal with everything else!

SOME ASSEMBLY REQUIRED

"For it was not an enemy that reproached me; then I could have borne it: neither was it he that hated me that did magnify himself against me; then I would have hid myself from him; But it was thou, a man mine equal, my guide, and mine acquaintance. We took sweet counsel together, and walked unto the house of God in company."

-- Psalm 55: 12-14

REGINA A. SOLLERS

"Yea, mine own familiar friend, in whom I trusted, which did eat of my bread, hath lifted up his heel against me."

-- Psalm 41:9

SOME ASSEMBLY REQUIRED

THE APPOINTMENT

The Appointment

There is an appointment we all must keep.
One day our Savior we will meet.
No rescheduling or cancellations allowed;
because of other engagements previously vowed.

Listen my friend time is far spent.
Only you know if you need to repent.
While you are alive work out your own salvation;
to ensure your residence within this Holy nation.

Don't be fooled—death is not the end.
Just like Lazarus you will rise again.
When you are called to stand before the King;
make sure your life is blameless and without sin.

"...prepare to meet thy God,..."

-- Amos 4:12

SOME ASSEMBLY REQUIRED

THE DRESS

The Dress

I'm clothed in beauty, like the first woman Eve.
I'm clothed in sorrow, like Hanna unable to conceive.

I'm clothed in determination, like Esther who went to see the King.
I'm clothed in meekness, like Ruth to her mother-in-law did cling.

I'm clothed in wisdom, like Deborah the prophetess and judge.
I'm clothed in faith, like the widow woman gave her last meal to Elijah and did not begrudge.

I'm clothed in submission, like Mary the handmaiden of the Lord.
I'm clothed in joy, like Elizabeth a son in her old age was a great reward.

I'm clothed in strength and honor, like the virtuous woman who excels them all.
I'm clothed in love, like the bride of Solomon awaiting in the banquet hall.

SOME ASSEMBLY REQUIRED

I'm clothed with God's Spirit, for He has dressed me well.
If there are things I lack, God will continue to clothe me and in His presence I will dwell.

Freedom for All

Jesus, my Lord, my Savior, my Redeemer.
Up on that Calvary cross He hung.
Bled, suffered, and died;
To set my poor soul free.

In my place He bore the cross.
Lovingly, He paid the price.
Each and every day I will thank Him;
Eternally grateful for His love!

Jubilee! Jubilee! I am now set free;
Because all of my sins were nailed to the tree.
Jubilee! Jubilee! Come children, come near.
Your freedom was bought.

IT'S THE JUBILEE YEAR!

(Written: July 24, 1999)

SOME ASSEMBLY REQUIRED

Some Assembly Required

You want a husband, there's nothing wrong with that.
For God said, "Marriage" is honorable and that's a fact.
But take care my sister—stand back and observe.
You need to be sure he's filled with God's word.
Otherwise, some assembly may be required.

Are you driving and riding and he's hiking and biking?
Do you have your own pad and he's still living with dad?
Take care my sister; don't be fooled by those good looks.
Make sure he's rooted and grounded in "The Good Book".
You see—some assembly may be required.

Are you working nine to five and he's home on the telephone line?
And when your check is due, he's borrowing from you.
Take care my sister; stop making excuses for the man.
Yes, pray for him—but leave him in God's hands.
Because some assembly may be required.

SOME ASSEMBLY REQUIRED

Remember that marriage is a lifetime commitment.
You want to be happy and filled with contentment.
Take care my sister; let God pick your mate;
to love, honor and cherish—for he's your lifelong date.
Beware of the brother where some assembly is required.

(Too many times we see the young sisters get caught up with a young man who doesn't have anything going for him but "looks". I wrote this poem because I see this situation too often and I want to encourage the young sisters to slow down; and let Jesus lead them.)

REGINA A. SOLLERS

LOVE POEMS

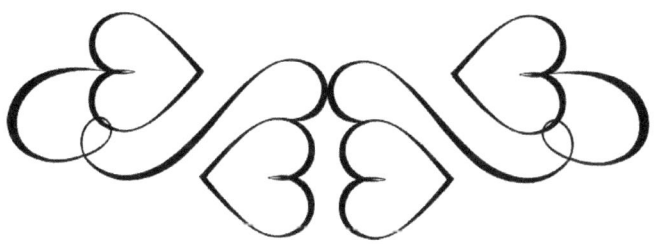

*"I am my beloved's,
and his desire is toward me."*

-- Song of Solomon 7:10

SOME ASSEMBLY REQUIRED

WE DID IT GOD'S WAY

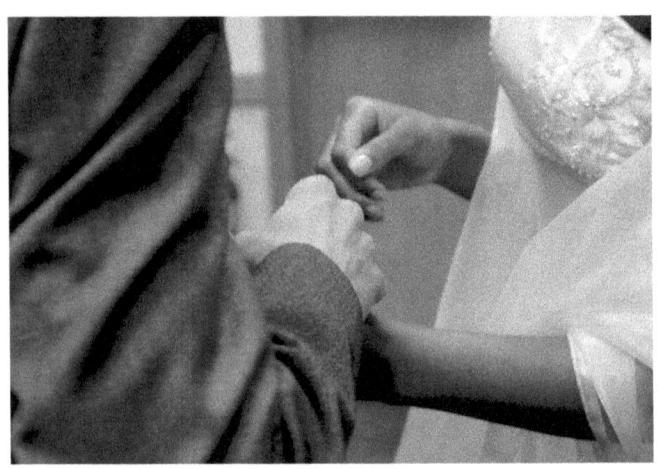

We Did it God's Way

We did it God's way and I'm so glad.
My life is full of joy, no reason to be sad.
I know you are my true soul mate.
Because we did it God's way; it was not fate.

When I look back over the years;
And remember our doubts and fears.
But through it all God has been true.
I am so glad I married you.

(This poem was inspired by a young couple who kept themselves pure and waited on the Lord to put them together.)

SOME ASSEMBLY REQUIRED

BLESSED LOVE

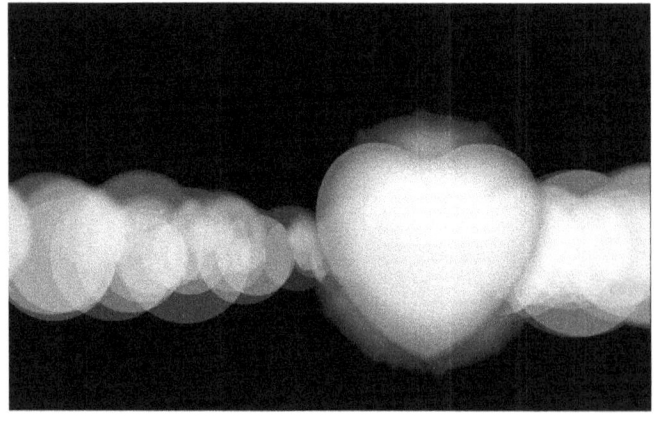

Blessed Love

God has blessed the love we have for

each other.

I long for you often, there could not

be another.

My desire is to you all of

the time.

You are my beloved, you are

my valentine.

(Inspired by the marriage of a deacon and his wife.)

SOME ASSEMBLY REQUIRED

I'M DRAWN TO YOU

I'm Drawn to You

Your eyes are like magnets, they draw me into your soul.
Your hands are so gentle, so beautiful to behold.
God created you such a beautiful creature.
Just for me. Just for me.

You're even more lovely with each passing day.
Lord, I thank you for my wife, on my knees I pray.
God created you such a beautiful being.
Just for me. Just for me.

You're so dear to me I cannot express how much.
My life has changed because of your touch.
God created you such a beautiful woman.
Just for me. Just for me.

SOME ASSEMBLY REQUIRED

ENDLESS LOVE

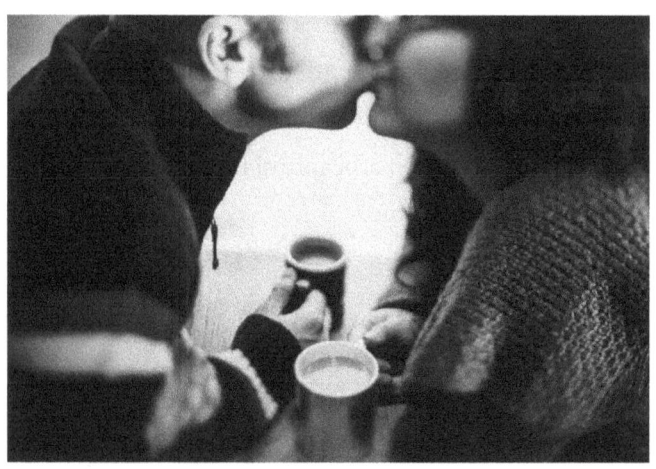

Endless Love

My love for you is still endless;
after all the years we've been together.
I would not change a thing in my life;
cause you are an exceptional and special fellow.

God has given me someone I can count on.
My sweet and wonderful guy.
I often think how truly blessed I am
While resting my head on you when night is nigh.

I love to be near you. I love to hold you.
You are my beloved—you are my heart.
You are my teddy bear and my strong tower.
God joined us together ne'er more to part.

SOME ASSEMBLY REQUIRED

I LOVE IT WHEN... *(the husband)*

I Love It When… *(the husband)*

I love it when
> you rub my head.

I love it when
> you say "Let's go to bed".

I love it when
> you snuggle under me at night.

I love it when
> you squeeze me tight.

I love it when
> you are home when I get there.

I love it when
> you do the little things that show you care.

I love it when
> you whisper my name.

I love it when
> you lightly touch my hand.

I love it when
> you smell so divine.

I love it when
> you look especially fine.

I love it when
> I smile at you and you smile back.

SOME ASSEMBLY REQUIRED

I love it when

    you even rub my neck, in fact.

I love it when

    you snuggle really close.

I love it when

    you kiss me—the most.

I love it when

    you say, I was on your mind all day.

I love it when

    you say, honey, it's time to steal away.

"Thy lips, O my spouse, drop as the honeycomb;"

-- Song of Solomon 3: 11

SOME ASSEMBLY REQUIRED

I LOVE IT WHEN... *(the wife)*

I Love It When... (*the wife*)

I love it when
> you stroke my hair.

I love it when
> you are here.

I love it when
> you pull me near.

I love it when
> you show me you care.

I love it when
> you hold me tight.

I love it when
> you kiss me goodnight.

I love it when
> you hold my hand.

I love it when
> you show me you understand.

I love it when
> you pleasantly smile.

I love it when
> you go the extra mile.

I love it when
> you and I embrace.

SOME ASSEMBLY REQUIRED

I love it when
    you kiss my face.

I love it when
    you and I are alone.
I love it when
    you whisper a sweet song.
I love it when
    you say "I love you".
I love it when
    you show me that you do.

"My beloved is like a roe or a young hart:…"

-- Song of Solomon 2:9

SOME ASSEMBLY REQUIRED

I AM MY BELOVED'S
and
MY BELOVED IS MINE

I Am My Beloved's and My Beloved Is Mine

(Song of Solomon 6:3)

Oh how sweet it is to trust in Jesus.
For I took Him at His word; and
He has given me my heart's desire.

How much more beautiful are the days
now that you are in them.
My beloved is mine, and I am my beloved.

Oh how I thank God for this day.
He answered my secret prayer;
and He has given me "whom my soul loveth".

Yes my beloved, today I am yours;
and yes, today you are mine.
We are no more twain—but one.

Amen! Amen! Amen!

(Written: 2000, The mother of the bride requested me to write a poem for her daughter's wedding.)

SOME ASSEMBLY REQUIRED

THE PROPOSAL

The Proposal

When I think of Adam in the Garden of Eden;
without any worries or cares.
Living a rich and a bountiful life;
it was oh so peaceful there.
He had everything one could ask for,
but sadly with no one to share.
God saw Adam's need - so he put Eve there.

God himself, said: "It's not good for man to be alone."
And I totally agree.
So that is why I want to ask you -
If you will marry me?

SOME ASSEMBLY REQUIRED

"Great is the Lord, and greatly to be praised…"

-- Psalm 48:1

TESTIMONIAL POEMS

*"I sought the Lord and He heard me,
and delivered me…"*

-- Psalm 34:4

SOME ASSEMBLY REQUIRED

GO FORWARD

Go Forward

What a beautiful and wonderful message
the Lord showed me one morning.
It was bright and early
before the break of the dawning.

On my way to work a cold, icy and wintry day.
Just a little slippery, as I made my way.
Rounded the curb and what a sight to behold.
Cars and trucks strewed across the road.

Go forward, the little voice said.
Oh no, I thought, so I delayed.
Vehicles turned around and some backed out.
As I continued to look, I began to have doubt.

So I decided I would turn around also.
But backward, God showed me I could not go.
What a mess I found myself in
when to God's voice I would not listen.

SOME ASSEMBLY REQUIRED

I tried to turn around but the car started to slide.
I begin to pray to God to be my guide.
"GO FORWARD" the voice did say.
I was obedient and God helped me on my way.

(Listen to God and stop looking at man. God has all power! When I decided to be obedient to God's voice, He helped me out of my situation. Thank you God for having mercy on me.)

IDLE WORDS

Be careful of your words

Idle Words

Let your "yea" be "yea" and your "nay" be "nay".
Because God who is in Heaven hears everything you say.
Be careful of the words that come from your mouth—
because you will live to regret them, there is no doubt.

Are you in a situation and wonder how you got that way.
Reexamine your life—maybe it's because of something you once said.
Off-handedly, in a moment of frustration or just casually.
Every idle word will be accountable, the Bible does decree.

I know first-hand how idle words can come back to haunt you.
I wanted to sell my house so badly; I didn't know what to do.
So out of my mouth came words that would bring me sorrow.
"If someone bought my house today, I'd move into an apartment tomorrow."

So God allowed these words to be so.
And into an apartment my family and I did go.
For 15 long months we suffered -
because of idle words I had uttered.

> *"That every idle word that men shall speak, they shall give account thereof in the day of judgment".*
>
> -- Matthew 12:36

(Remember, many times your idle words involves someone else that has to suffer too.)

SOME ASSEMBLY REQUIRED

GOD IS A TEACHER

God Is A Teacher

God is a teacher; I know this to be true.
When you need help just ask him,
He'll tell you what to do.

When I needed to get the lawn mower into my car—
He showed me an old table in the garage afar.
Place it on the bumper so that it will incline.
And the lawn mower I got into the car just fine.

Not only has He taught me but He has taught others -
how to care for their spouses, fathers and mothers.
We can do nothing unless God allows us to.
When you need help just ask, He will tell you what to do.

Obey God Right Now

It is a good thing to be obedient to the Lord.
His grace and mercy will be your reward.
Don't hesitate when God is talking to you.
Don't rationalize what you should do.

Remember God's ways are not our ways.
His time is not counted by days.
Decide right now to be instant in and out of season.
If God tells you to, then you don't need a reason.

Make up your mind to obey God right now.
And what a blessed friend you will have found.
Obedience is indeed better than a sacrifice.
Obey God right now, He may not tell you twice.

Obey – The Biblical word for "obey" comes from the Greek *"hupakou"* which means to listen attentively; by implication to heed or conform to a command of authority. This word conveys the idea of actively following a command. There is no choice in the matter, it is to be done whether one agrees with it or not. Obedience is involuntary.

What Christians † Want to Know

By: Pamela Rose Williams

ABOUT THE AUTHOR

I accepted Christ as Lord and Savior of my life February 1994; and it was the best decision I ever made. When I speak the name "Jesus" a smile bursts forth in my spirit. He truly is my joy and refuge.

My passion for writing developed early in life while I was in high school. It is my desire that all who read my material be encourage and gain a greater spiritual insight into their own lives. Many of the poems in this book were inspired by others' testimonies, sermons I heard and my own experiences.

Most of my working years were spent in the federal government Department of Treasury Bureau of Engraving and Printing. During my tenure there, I served in many capacities and thoroughly enjoyed the time I spent there and the wonderful people I met and worked with. After 38 years I retired as Supervisor Accountability Help Desk. God said it was time to go and to do more for Him. Since then I have been on mission trips to Guatemala, Jamaica and Kenya. I am also the Director of the Lothian Church of God's Benevolent Ministry where we prepare dinner monthly for the residents at the Annapolis Lighthouse Shelter. I am responsible, too, for preparing Thanksgiving and Christmas holiday baskets and distributing backpacks and school supplies.

God is the center of my life, my joy and MY SHEPHERD.

REGINA A. SOLLERS

TO CONTACT THE AUTHOR

Regina A. Sollers
iigi4me@verizon.net
regina.sollers@facebook.com
www.iigi4me.com
P.O. Box 128
Cheltenham, Maryland 20623

TO PURCHASE ADDITIONAL BOOKS:

www.teachablemomentspress.com

www.iigi4me.com

www.amazon.com

Also available on Kindle

Ingram Distribution

Published by:
Teachable Moments Press
6030 Marshalee Drive, #175
Elkridge, MD 21075
443-251-2911

NOTES

FOR PERSONAL REFLECTION

NOTES

FOR PERSONAL REFLECTION

NOTES

FOR PERSONAL REFLECTION

NOTES

FOR PERSONAL REFLECTION

NOTES

FOR PERSONAL REFLECTION

www.ingramcontent.com/pod-product-compliance
Lightning Source LLC
Chambersburg PA
CBHW071154090426
42736CB00012B/2332